God, I Need to Talk to You about SCHOOL

SIGH

Written by Susan K. Leigh
Pictures by Bill Clark

CONCORDIA PUBLISHING HOUSE · SAINT LOUIS

Dear God,
I don't like **school**.
And I don't want to
go any more.

I don't want to go because I'm **not very good** at school. Other kids are better. Sometimes I just don't understand things.

Apply your heart to instruction and your ear to words of knowledge.

Proverbs 23:12

Mom said that everybody
has to go to school. She said
there's no other way. She asked
me what the **problem** was.

I told her that Kaitlyn made fun of me because I didn't know the math answers and she did. That's why **I don't want to go** to school anymore.

I told her that Mrs. Cooper **helps me** at recess. I don't want to stay in at recess. I want to go outside to play with my friends.

Mom said she was sorry about
Kaitlyn. She said it was good that Mrs.
Cooper was helping me and she and Dad
would help me too. And she said she was
certain that I would catch on.

That made me feel **better**.

Know that wisdom is such to your soul; if you find it, there will be a future.

Proverbs 24:14

Mom said **I can pray to You** anytime I feel upset about school. She said that would help me feel better so I can focus on learning.

I know that will work because You always hear our prayers in Jesus' name. So, Lord, would You help me enjoy school more? Would You help me learn?